Drea

the musical

Jo Noel-Hartley

A SAMUEL FRENCH ACTING EDITION

SAMUEL FRENCH
FOUNDED 1830

SAMUELFRENCH.COM
SAMUELFRENCH-LONDON.CO.UK

ISBN 978-0-573-18011-8

www.SamuelFrench.com
www.SamuelFrench-London.co.uk

For Production Enquiries

United States and Canada
Info@SamuelFrench.com
1-866-598-8449

United Kingdom and Europe
Theatre@SamuelFrench-London.co.uk
020-7255-4302

Each title is subject to availability from Samuel French, depending upon country of performance. Please be aware that *DREAM STREET* may not be licensed by Samuel French in your territory. Professional and amateur producers should contact the nearest Samuel French office or licensing partner to verify availability.

DREAM STREET was first produced by the Jam Theatre Company's JammEd Theatre School in Marlow, Buckinghamshire on 8th July 2008. The performance was directed by Jo Noel-Hartley, choreographed by Tom Dwyer and production managed by Mark Hartley. The cast was as follows:

HUGO FINCH .... Harry Radcliffe
MAGGIE FINCH .... Evangeline Cullingworth
RUPERT FINCH .... James Hayward
CHARLIE .... Simon Page
JEMIMA .... Fiona Simms
ERIC .... Ozzie Gardner
HEATHER .... Amy Donegan
LILY .... Eloise Grohs
TOM .... Will Spratley
LAURA .... Hannah Hutchinson
LUCAS .... Toby Eastwood
GEORGE .... Ollie Murray
SPARKLE MOON .... Ella Casale
LETICIA MOON .... Andrea Newland
SEBASTIAN RICKTER .... Steve Dula
JESS .... Victoria Scambler
JACKSON .... Nicola Page
MRS DEWBERRY .... Alice Bennett
MARJORIE .... Hannah Walker
JESSE .... Ryan Noel-Hartley
EDWARD .... Sam Hayward
SOPHIE .... Sophie Paton
DANIEL .... Ollie Murray
STEPHANIE .... Eleanor Mallon
OSCAR .... James Robbins
COMPANY .... JammEd Theatre School Students

CHARACTERS

LEAD ROLES

HUGO FINCH, 11 year old son of parents trying to be very 'upper class' and enforcing this on their son. Nice boy, but confused as to who he is and what he wants.
MAGGIE FINCH, Hugo's mum. Always trying to keep up with the Jones'. Drives a 4 x 4, wears a scarf around her neck, is on the PTA of Hugo's school, and member of the elite tennis club. She is desperate for status.
RUPERT FINCH, Hugo's dad. Works in the city, very successful, member of an exclusive gentlemen's club which the producer of the show is also a member.

CHARLIE, aged 10. Really nice boy who loves football. Supportive, easy going parents, ('as long as he's happy' kind of thing). His school teacher sees his potential as a natural performer and encourages him to audition.

JEMIMA, aged 13, lives with mum and granddad. Humble and kind, bit hippy-ish in style. Likes reading, bit sheltered due to being only child. Goes to a small village hall ballet class, not the trendy ones!
ERIC, Jemima's granddad. Has stepped in as father figure. Retired and keeps things together. Quite wise.
HEATHER, Jemima's mum. Single Mother. Bit hippy-ish too. Worked off her feet to pay bills. Always running around.

LILY, blonde haired little cutie, aged 11. Loves singing, dancing, acting and has classes nearly every day! Must be a good tap dancer. Has been to loads of auditions but never got anywhere. Has two younger brothers who annoy her. Doesn't know her parents are getting divorced.
TOM, Lily's dad. Handsome, nice guy, good dad.
LAURA, Lily's cool mum. Has 3 kids, lively, about to separate from Tom.
LUCAS, Lily's oldest brother.
GEORGE, Lily's youngest brother.

SPARKLE MOON, a 12-year-old stage school darling. Has been attending a top stage school since she was 3. Has had extra work in some TV and film, thanks to her pushy mum who is also her agent. Is talented though and not as nightmarish as her mother.
LETICIA MOON, Sparkle's mother. Has devoted her life to see Sparkle become a star. Seems to be oblivious to everyone around her and is a law unto herself. Sparkle's potential downfall, rather than asset.

SEBASTIAN RICKTER, world renowned director and producer for theatre. Has won awards. Flamboyant in appearance and nature. Seems to have an air of not caring for anyone but himself, but this is an act.

NAMED ROLES WITH LINES AND/OR SONGS

JESS, Main casting director. Really good at her job and kind with it.
CASSIE, Second casting director. A little less friendly than Jess.
RACHEL, Casting assistant. One spoken line, but in most audition scenes.
JACKSON, Brilliant dancer and choreographer of the show.
MRS DEWBERRY, Dear old lady, who is well established vocal coach in the industry. Wears glasses around her neck and a bad taste in clothes. Very sweet though, and knows what she is doing.
MARJORIE, Mrs Dewberry's long-standing pianist. Doesn't say any lines, but must be a good comedy actress to act alongside Mrs Dewberry.
CHARLIE'S MUM, never seen, only shouts 'Charlie!' in scene 1B.

JESSE, the boy who finally gets the main part in the show. Must be an excellent actor with comic timing and excellent singing voice for final song.
EDWARD, auditioning boy who does monologue with Jesse
SOPHIE, auditioning girl who sings a solo song brilliantly in front of Mrs Dewberry. She should be a strong dancer and singer as she will be in the final song.
DANIEL, auditioning boy, aged 12/13, who's voice is starting to break. Sings a solo comic song in the auditions where his voice is breaking, must be happy to laugh at himself.
STEPHANIE, auditioning girl who tries to sing the song *Amazing Grace.* Doesn't have to be a strong singer but must be an excellent comic actress.
OSCAR, auditioning boy, who has a small acting monologue during the auditions.
SAM, auditioning boy who has a solo line in first song.
CHILD, any child who is auditioning and has one line of dialogue in Act 1 Scene 2.
MIA, auditioning girl who does not say anything but is named in the acting auditions. It is therefore assumed she is good enough to make it through to the final castings.

COMPANY

Any number of children auditioning for the show. As the musical progresses the size of the company steadily reduces, making it easier to rehearse specific songs and scenes with potentially a very large cast. Some of the cast could be mainly dancers who sing, especially with the tap audition.

SETTING

Various simple settings

IMPORTANT BILLING AND CREDIT REQUIREMENTS

If you have obtained performance rights to this title, please refer to your licensing agreement for important billing and credit requirements.

SONG LIST

1.	Maybe Today	Company
2.	Maybe Today (Reprise)	Company
3.	Dreams Can Come True	Company
4.	My Love Is Here To Stay	Sophie
5.	Amazing Grace	Stephanie
6.	Little Bird	Sparkle
7.	Tell Me	Jemima
8.	Keep The Heart Within Our Home	Tom and Laura
9.	Gotta Give In To The Music	Company
10.	Feel The Rhythm	Company
11.	Life Is What You Make It	Company
12.	Dreams Can Come True (Reprise)	Company
13.	Tomorrow, Today	Company
14.	Life Is What You Make It (Reprise)	Company
14.	Feel The Rhythm (Reprise)	Company

Backing tracks and lead sheets are available on hire from Samuel French. Please enquire.

Additional staging information and resources are available online at www.jamtheatre.co.uk

AUTHOR'S NOTE

Dream Street was created mainly because I had a large teenage cast of 80, and couldn't find a show that wasn't "four leads plus chorus"! Our students were a real mixed bunch of talent: some more singers than dancers, others more dancers than singers, some just super strong actors... and I wanted to showcase as many as possible!

As you can see from the extensive cast list, by writing my own show I was able to showcase a lot more than just a few leads. It was a huge undertaking, but one of the most memorable times in my career. Even several years on, the now near-adults are still singing the songs and even remember the routines! And that's what I wanted really — the lyrics in particular for *Life Is What You Make It, Dreams Can Come True, Tomorrow Today* and *Keep the Heart Within Our Home,* all have messages to live by.

I hope if you are considering using this show for your own students, when you read through you will see its potential and enjoy it as much as we did.

Jo Noel-Hartley

To all the talented cast, crew and staff that were involved in the first ever performance of DREAM STREET (JammEd/Jam Theatre Company UK)

... thanks SO much for sharing your talent, trusting me and taking a risk on a brand new show! You were awesome!

ACT ONE

(Outskirts of Greater London, a suburb of Clemenston, Spring. Current day. 4pm on a Friday afternoon, last day of school term.)

*(MUSIC: **"OVERTURE"**)*

(Somewhere at the edge of the stage must be a street sign, which shows the corner of Dean Street and Stratton Way.)

*(We see the front door of 4 homes, all characteristic of their families. The 4 houses are all on Dean Street. The 4 houses span the full length of the road with No. 4 (***HUGO***'s house) being at the posh end and No. 142 (***JEMIMA***'s house) being at a run-down cheaper end of the suburb.)*

*(***HUGO*** has been at home all day as he goes to private school, and finished term early. He's very bored, and sitting outside, hoping to watch the kids walk by after school simply to add some interest to his day.)*

(School kids are skipping home, different uniforms, mums, push chairs, university students, local gardener...)

*(An elderly gentleman in a raincoat (***ERIC***) walks down the road (stage left to right) reading the paper. He stops, having seen something interesting, then continues off stage to collect ***JEMIMA*** from school. When we see him again, he has a newspaper under his arm, fresh bread for tea, and is clearly chatting to ***JEMIMA*** about her day – having a laugh. He picks a flower out of ***HUGO***'s garden to give to ***JEMIMA***. ***HUGO***'s mum ***MAGGIE*** is looking through the window with her marigolds on, face*

like thunder. She comes outside to collect **HUGO** *and save him from the 'hobo'. She drags him inside.)*

*(***LILY*** is walking home with her friends from school, maybe listening to an iPod (sharing it with another girl) and doing a few dance moves to it. She waves goodbye to her friends, does a little dance routine to what she's listening to before she goes inside.)*

*(***CHARLIE*** and two friends (***JOE*** and ***OSCAR***) are kicking a football to each other before* **CHARLIE** *waves them goodbye and goes inside.)*

(Busy-ness of street slows down, lights change as evening comes, and the last people we see are **JEMIMA***'s mum* **HEATHER** *rushing into No. 142 with a zillion bags in her hand, after an exhausting days work...and* **HUGO***'s dad* **RUPERT** *in smart suit and briefcase, turns around to alarm his posh car, and enters No 4.)*

(Music finishes and we open in **LILY***'s house, around the Dinner table with* **LILY***, Mum* **LAURA***, Dad* **TOM** *and two younger brothers* **LUCAS** *and* **GEORGE***)*

Scene 1A

TOM. *(in between mouthfuls)* I'm sorry I've got to work these holidays guys, but a least you're all busy doing stuff you'll enjoy!

LUCAS. *(excitedly)* Yeah computer tech camp!

GEORGE. *(grumpy)* I'd rather stay here and play on my playstation all week.

LAURA. *(encouraging)* Come on George, you say that every year and end up loving it more than Lucas!

TOM. Are you excited about the audition on Monday Lil?

LILY. Yeah! Can't wait! Miss Sarah's been really emphasising the value of attending auditions like this, to get our experience up. But this show is going to be HUGE!

LAURA. You'll be in your element singing and dancing all week.

LILY. *(practically bursting)* I KNOW!

(Cross fade to **CHARLIE***'s house.)*

(MUSIC: Scene Change)

Scene 1B

*(**CHARLIE**'s on the phone to his mate **OSCAR**, who's also going to the audition.)*

CHARLIE. ...yeh... I know. At least you've got more experience than me, Oscar. I've never done this before! ...uh huh... Too right... No, I'm not gonna let Mrs Jacobs down. She's asked me to give it a try, and I'm a man of my word... Well, boy anyway!

MUM. *(off stage)* Charlie!

CHARLIE. Listen, gotta go. My dinner's ready. So I'll see you there Monday... Yeh... Cheers, mate.

*(**CHARLIE** hangs up the phone and exits towards his dining room.)*

*(Fade to **HUGO**'s house)*

(MUSIC: Scene Change)

Scene 1C

*(***HUGO*** and his mum ***MAGGIE*** and dad ***RUPERT*** are sitting around having a drink before dinner.)*

MAGGIE. Hugo? Come and sit down with us for a minute.

*(***HUGO*** is curious but obedient.)*

Daddy has an amazing opportunity for you next week. Rupert?

RUPERT. Thank you, darling. Yes, Hugo. How would *you* like to audition to be in a West End show?

(Mum and Dad's faces are brimming with excitement as they both sit on the edges of their seats. **HUGO** *doesn't react)*

MAGGIE. Did you hear your father, Hugo? A West End show!!!

HUGO. *(looking very puzzled)* But I can't dance or act...or sing really.

RUPERT. It's not about skill, Hugo darling, they'll teach you all that on the job. It's about having the right 'look'... *(to* **MAGGIE***)* and knowing the right people doesn't hurt either!

(They laugh together then suddenly stop.)

MAGGIE. Hugo, darling, I think it would be great for you. Will you give it a try? The auditions are on Monday.

HUGO. *(thinks for a minute)* ... OK. If you think so.

RUPERT. That's my boy.

(Fade to **JEMIMA***'s house)*

(MUSIC: Scene Change)

Scene 1D

*(***ERIC***,* **HEATHER** *and* **JEMIMA** *are all having a cup of tea after dinner.* **ERIC** *puts an open newspaper in front of* **JEMIMA***.)*

JEMIMA. What's this, Grandad?

ERIC. Read the bottom right hand corner.

JEMIMA. *(picking up the paper, she reads)* 'Sebastian Rickter, world famous director, invites boys and girls aged nine to thirteen to audition for his new West End Musical "DREAM STREET". Open auditions take place at 9 a.m. on Monday 11th April, at Whitfield Studios, Clemenston. Successful audtionees must be available for the entire week, and for the months of June to December 2008 should they be chosen to star in the show.'

So?

ERIC. I think you should go for it.

JEMIMA. What? It's THIS MONDAY! You're mad. I haven't got enough experience. And I'm not the right kind of person for this kind of thing.

HEATHER. What's the 'right kind of person'?

JEMIMA. You know, pretty, bubbly, confident, can sing, dance and act, – and must have great teeth!

ERIC. You can dance and sing, and probably act too. Your teachers always say how talented you are.

JEMIMA. Mum?

HEATHER. There's no harm in giving it a go, Jem. What else were you planning on doing these holidays? You know I've got to work. Do you really want to hang around with this old codger all week?! *(directed to* **ERIC***)*

ERIC. *(light-hearted)* Hey! Respect the old man!

JEMIMA. I s'pose not – No offence, Grandad! It's your idea after all. *(pause, thinking)* Yeh... OK *(She is more upbeat about it. She looks at newspaper again)* YEH, why not? If

Sebastian Rickter is coming to Clemenston, maybe he wants someone local and plain.

*(***ERIC** *&* **HEATHER** *roll their eyes and look at each other.)*

ERIC & HEATHER. You're anything but plain!

(All laugh. Fade to Black.)

(MUSIC: Scene Change)

(During the scene change **LILY, CHARLIE, HUGO** *and* **JEMIMA** *are highlighted in spotlights with their bags ready for the first day of auditions.)*

Scene 2

*(SONG: **MAYBE TODAY**)*

(It is Monday morning when children are arriving to the audition. As the song continues, more and more children arrive with their parents and join in singing until it's the whole cast. **HUGO** *is wearing a 3-piece suit)*

(Towards the end of the song we meet super-confident **SPARKLE MOON** *followed closely behind by her mother* **LETICIA**.*)*

(The song continues while we see the kids all lining up outside the audition room, get registered in, labelled with number and wait for their next instruction.)

COMPANY.

MAYBE TODAY'S THE DAY I GET MY BREAKTHOUGH.
MAYBE TODAY'S THE DAY I'LL BE A STAR.
MAYBE TODAY'S THE DAY I'M NOT REJECTED,
OR GET MY HOPES UP TOO FAR.

MAYBE TODAY THEY'LL NOTICE WHAT I'M WEARING.
MAYBE TODAY MY VOICE WON'T LET ME DOWN.
MAYBE TODAY I'LL GET THE DANCE ROUTINE RIGHT,
OR END UP LOOKING A CLOWN.

WHY DO I PUT MYSELF THOUGH ALL THIS AGONY?
(WAH WAH WAH)
OPEN AUDITIONS ARE THE WORST.
I HOPE THIS NUMBER WON'T LOOK BAD ON ME.

SAM.

DON'T GIVE ME THIRTEEN OR I'M CURSED.

COMPANY.

MAYBE TODAY IS ONLY THE BEGINNING.
MAYBE TODAY THEY'LL SEE WHAT I CAN DO.
MAYBE TODAY'S THE DAY THAT I'LL BE WINNING,
OH I HOPE I GET THROUGH.

OH I HOPE. (OH I HOPE.)
OH I HOPE. (OH I HOPE.)
OH I HOPE.

JEMIMA.

MAYBE TODAY I'LL FIND OUT WHAT I'M GOOD AT.

CHARLIE.

MAYBE TODAY I'LL LEARN A THING OR TWO.

HUGO & CHARLIE.

MAYBE TODAY'S THE MORNING HE WILL LIKE ME,
OH I HOPE IT COMES TRUE.

LILY.

MAYBE TODAY I'LL STAND OUT FROM THE OTHERS.
MAYBE TODAY I'LL LOOK RIGHT FOR THE PART.

COMPANY.

MAYBE TODAY THOSE LESSONS WILL BE WORTH IT,
I HOPE I DON'T FALL APART.

WHY DO I PUT MYSELF THROUGH ALL THIS AGONY?
(WAH WAH WAH)
ALL FOR A LITTLE SLICE OF FAME.
I'M DESTINED FOR THE STAGE; IT'S PART OF ME.
WON'T STOP 'TILL THE BILLBOARD'S GOT MY NAME.

COS THAT MOMENT IN THE SPOTLIGHT
MAKES THE AGONY WORTHWHILE.
THAT MOMENT WHEN THE GLORY IS ALL YOURS.
YOU SWEAT, YOU GRIND, YOU TRAIN YOURSELF AND
STILL YOU WEAR A SMILE.
JUST TO HEAR. (JUST TO HEAR) JUST TO HEAR.
THE ROAR OF YOUR APPLAUSE.

MAYBE TODAY.
MAYBE TODAY.
MAYBE TODAY.

(Song ends.)

JESS. *(loudly)* Can I have your attention please? *(She waits for the commotion to calm down)* Thank you all for coming to today's open audition to work with world-famous director Sebastian Rickter. My name is Jess and I'll be looking after you today.

You will now be handed some notes that will help you with your audition. It is very important that you read them all. There is also a short passage of script that we would like you to learn. We will pair you up with another auditionee when you do that scene later on. But for now, make yourself comfortable and we will call you when we're ready.

Please have your CVs to hand if you have one. *(Exit)*

(Mild panic for those kids who are auditioning for the first time. **LILY** *has one and ruffles through her bag.* **SPARKLE** *displays her 'larger than life' photo and CV with ribbon around it.)*

(Children are reading through the notes, warming up their voices, doing some stretches, playing cards, reading books etc...)

(We see **JEMIMA** *and* **LILY** *strike up a friendship.)*

JEMIMA. *(talking to herself)* I don't have a CV. Why would I have a CV?

LILY. Don't worry, you don't have to have one.

JEMIMA. Sorry?

LILY. CV. It's OK if you don't have one. I'm Lily.

JEMIMA. Hi. I'm Jemima. Are you sure I don't need a CV?

LILY. Absolutely. I've been to loads of these things. If they like you, you'll get through with or without one. Your first time?

JEMIMA. Obvious huh? My grandad saw the ad in the paper, and thought I should give it a go.

LILY. Cool. My theatre school teacher makes us go to every audition – says it's good experience. Do you go to stage school?

JEMIMA. No, but I do attend ballet classes. Have done since I was three. And I'm in the school choir.

LILY. You'll be fine then. Don't worry. I'm sure it mentioned strong dance skills in the letter. My problem is if you look around, I bet ninety percent of these kids go to some kind of stage school and can all sing, dance and act. At least with you, you're a bit quirky, a bit different. Directors love that.

(We fade out from this conversation into listening to **SPARKLE***'s conversation.)*

(She is the centre of attention surrounded by 'groupies' who are being taken in by her every word. She has a mini photo album in her hand.)

SPARKLE. ... *(showing a photo)* And this was when I played 'Child Number Four' in the documentary about the making of Dr Who. If you look closely you can see David Tennant there in the corner... See? ...well, it's not him exactly, but a life-size cardboard cut out... but anyway... here, I played 'injured girl on road' in *Casualty*, and in this photo you can see the back of my hair... *(fade out)*

(We head over to see **CHARLIE**. *He has a tennis ball that he keeps bouncing against the wall. He's trying to learn his words at the same time. The ball hits* **HUGO** *by mistake.)*

CHARLIE. I'm SO SO sorry mate. Gosh, what was I thinking. Please forgive me. I clearly can't multitask! The name's Charlie Harris. *(puts his hand out to shake* **HUGO***s)*

HUGO. *(mumbling)* ...No problem... um... I'm Hugo. Hugo Finch.

CHARLIE. Nice to meet you Hugo Finch. Ever done one of these auditions before? I haven't. First timer, me. How I'm meant to memorise all these words, I don't know. I'm dyslexic, so who knows how it's gonna come out! *(light-hearted)* Will give it me best shot!

My English teacher reckons I've got something... some 'Inner Charm' she reckons. Can you see it, Hugo? *(***CHARLIE** *poses in a silly model pose)* Can you see my 'inner charm'?

(They burst into laughter together)

So how'd you get here?

HUGO. Mummy and Daddy's idea really. I'm not sure I really fit in... I mean look at me! *(referring to his clothes)* I could help you learn your lines if you'd like.

CHARLIE. Thanks, but shouldn't you worry about learning your own?

HUGO. I've learnt mine already. I've been blessed with a photographic memory.

CHARLIE. Lucky you!

HUGO. But I've also got two left feet, so if I get through today I'll be a great source of amusement in the dance auditions!

(Both boys laugh, and sit down to go through **CHARLIE***'s lines.* **JESS** *enters and interrupts everyone by calling numbers, collecting those numbered kids into the next room for their audition.)*

JESS. Right everyone. Can I have your attention please?Can the following numbers please come and stand in an orderly line here in front of Rachel. Numbers 126 through to 140. That's any number between 126 up to and including 140.

(Children look to see what number they are. Those chosen from a queue, some scared, some confident.)

CHILD. *(puts her hand up)* Is that me? I don't know if that's me.

*(***JESS** *looks at the crumpled-up paper)*

JESS. Yes that means you. *(kindly)* You may need to pay a little more attention in your maths lesson!

RACHEL. OK, everyone. Follow me.

CHARLIE. *(genuinely, to everyone)* Good luck!

(Everyone looks at **CHARLIE** *as if he's an alien!)*

CHARLIE. What? *(not sure why they're looking at him)*

*(***RACHEL** *leads the group out into another room. Everyone watches as they leave, and the reality sets in for those remaining.)*

(Lights fade.)

Scene 3

*(SONG: **MAYBE TODAY** Reprise)*

(During the song we see all of the children collecting letters telling them whether they got through the day's castings. There are pink letters for unsuccessful and green for successful kids. We see all our main characters.)

COMPANY.

MAYBE TODAY'S THE DAY I GET MY BREAKTHOUGH.
MAYBE TODAY'S THE DAY I'LL BE A STAR.
MAYBE TODAY'S THE DAY I'M NOT REJECTED,
OR GET MY HOPES UP TOO FAR.

MAYBE TODAY IS ONLY THE BEGINNING.
MAYBE TODAY THEY'LL SEE WHAT I CAN DO.
MAYBE TODAY'S THE DAY THAT I'LL BE WINNING,
OH I HOPE I GET THROUGH.

WHY DO I PUT MYSELF THOUGH ALL THIS AGONY?
(WAH WAH WAH)
OPEN AUDITIONS CLEARLY STINK.
I WANTED THIS SO VERY BADLY.

PINK KIDS.

I WORKED MY BUTT OFF AND GOT PINK!

GREEN KIDS.

GOT THROUGH TODAY I REALLY CAN'T BELIEVE IT.
WHAT CAN I SAY THIS ROLE IS NEARLY MINE.
GOT THROUGH TODAY I REALLY DID ACHIEVE IT.
TOMORROW I'M GONNA SHINE.

*(**SPARKLE** walks past with her papers in hand (showing them off) talking on her mobile to her mum about the audition, handbag, scarf, very confident.)*

SPARKLE. Yes mummy... Aha... Absolutely!!.... aha... of course I got through, Mummy!!... yes… well I'm just going to grab a latte… say five to ten minutes… love you. *(fade out)*

(During this rush of people walking across stage, the set changes to the inside of Jemima and Lily's houses only as **JEMIMA** *gets closer to her front door.)*

Scene 3A

JEMIMA. *(entering the kitchen)* Grandad!

(She puts down her bags. She puts her papers down and slumps into the kitchen chair exhausted. Grandad kisses her on the cheek.)

JEMIMA. It was the best day EVER! The weirdest experience I've ever had!

ERIC. *(making them both a cup of tea)* Here, darling. Tell me everything! *(sitting down at kitchen table)*

JEMIMA. Well, after you dropped me off, I was really nervous at first, didn't recognise anyone at all. I met a really lovely girl called Lily. She's done loads of auditions, but she was really nice and kind to me. I wasn't so worried after I met her. *(She eats a biscuit and continues talking)*

Sooooo many kids had much more experience than me, like Lily. There was this one girl, called Sparkle – I thought *my* name was weird! – and she seems to have done every TV show there is. She's so confident, it's scary!

ERIC. Yes, but is she talented?

JEMIMA. Yeh... I think she is! *(eats another biscuit)*

ERIC. *(looking at his watch)* Your mum will be back any minute now. She'll want to know very detail! *(picks up the recall letter)* What's this?

JEMIMA. *(proudly)* I got called back tomorrow!

*(**ERIC** and **JEMIMA** hug and jump around the room as **HEATHER** enters carrying lots of bags. **HEATHER** looks tired, has obviously been working long hours, but manages to be excited for her daughter.)*

HEATHER. What's this I'm seeing?! Has my baby girl done well today? *(Hugs **JEMIMA**, kisses her on the head)* Did you enjoy yourself darling?

JEMIMA. Mum, I loved it. It was fascinating watching everyone... and I learnt so much... And scary at the same time. And Mum... I got recalled! They want me back tomorrow!

HEATHER. That's fantastic. Good on you. *(she holds* **JEMIMA***'s head in her hands)* This family finally has a star in the making! I don't want you to have to work as hard as I have to, honey. You deserve so much more. Let's have a toast! *(pours apple juice into some cups, they all stand ready for the toast)* Here's to a successful round two.

ALL 3. To round two! *(all clink glasses)*

(Fade to **LILY***'s house.)*

(MUSIC: Scene Change)

Scene 3B

(We're now instantly in **LILY***'s house. Both* **LILY***'s parents,* **TOM** *&* **LAURA** *are there.)*

LAURA. Darling, that's fantastic! When's the recall? *(***LILY** *hands her the letters, which* **LAURA** *reads quickly).* Tomorrow! Wow they're not mucking around. That's great.

LILY. Yep, and if I get through, rehearsals start June 16th. So I would have finished my exams by then, and of course, you'll have to sign permission for me to miss school. I think they have a tutor as part of the team. Pretty cool heh?

(As **LILY** *has been chatting,* **TOM** *and* **LAURA** *have been looking at each other with a concerned look.)*

TOM. Were there many of your friends there?

LILY. *(making herself a cup of tea)* Yeh, the usual Saturday crowd. Met a really nice girl though, called Jemima. Oh and guess who else was there?

ALL 3. *(said in perfect time)* Sparkle Moon! *(all laugh)*

TOM. You mean to tell me she hasn't had her 'big Hollywood break' yet? With a mother like hers, I'm surprised she's not running for presidency!

LILY. *(laughs)* Well, it would be funny if she wasn't so damn good at what she does! Anyway, with vocal lessons tomorrow, I'd better get a move on and do some practice!

*(***LILY** *heads off to her bedroom upstairs.)*

LAURA. While you're up there, can you tell the boys dinner won't be too much longer? And Lily... *(***LILY** *stops and pokes her head around to hear her mum)* ...well done, honey. We're proud of you.

LILY. Thanks, Mum.

*(***LILY** *Exits.* **TOM** *&* **LAURA** *continue their conversation in a stage whisper.)*

LAURA. What are we going to do, Tom? This is her dream. If she does get through, her rehearsals will be right in the middle of... *(deep intake of breath)* ... How do we keep it from her then, too?

(Lights fade.)

(MUSIC: Scene Change)

Scene 4

(Day 2 of auditions: singing auditions. In a separate studio, we see sitting next to a piano an older lady called **MRS DEWBERRY**. *She wears glasses that are on a chain around her neck. She's a cuddly woman with dreadful taste in clothes and probably owns lots of cats. Behind the piano is an overly-enthusiastic rehearsal pianist, also slightly older, called Marjorie. We see a portion of the children in this room, but can still see the rest of the kids in the holding room.)*

MRS DEWBERRY. Good morning, darlings.

SPARKLE. *(very quickly and loudly)* Good morning Mrs Dewberry. *(loud whisper to anyone who'll listen)* She is amazing, I have private lessons sometimes with her in London. She trains all the West End Stars.

MRS DEWBERRY. Congratulations on making it through to day two. As you can see, there aren't as many of you here today as there were yesterday, and there will be less of you tomorrow... but you *must* remember you are here *(slight pause)* because you have *talent*. Let's see what we can get out of you today.

Now... How many of you have singing lessons?

(Some put up their hands. **SPARKLE***'s arm stretches the highest.)*

MRS DEWBERRY. Wonderful. Let's see what you know, and those of you who haven't, don't worry. Sometimes it's easier to start with a blank canvas.

We'll start with breathing. Who can demonstrate how to breathe correctly?

*(***SPARKLE** *jumps up, eager to demonstrate.)*

MRS DEWBERRY. Very well, dear, let's have a look.

(Fade to black as **SPARKLE** *demonstrates breathing...)*

(Lights up again to reveal we're about an hour further into the lesson. The children have been learning the opening number of the show, and are all singing it.)

(SONG: ***DREAMS CAN COME TRUE*** *(Short Version))*

COMPANY.

DREAMS CAN COME TRUE ANY DAY,
DREAMS CAN COME TRUE ANYWHERE.
JUST HOLD ON TIGHT AND BE READY TO FLY ANYWHERE
YOUR DREAMS WILL TAKE YOU
DREAMS CAN COME TRUE ANY TIME
DREAMS ONLY NEED AN OPEN MIND
WHAT IS LIFE WITHOUT A DREAM TO DREAM?

*(***JESS*** and ***CASSIE*** enter during the number with their clipboards.)*

(At the end of the song...)

MRS DEWBERRY. That's lovely. I think we all have that now. OK? Now, dears, it's time to hear you sing individually. Who'd like to go first?

*(***SPARKLE*** puts her hand up eagerly, But ***MRS DEWBERRY*** chooses ***SOPHIE***. ***SOPHIE*** passes her sheet music to the pianist. ***JEMIMA*** starts to panic as she didn't know she had to bring music. ***SPARKLE*** gets her sheet music ready.)*

MRS DEWBERRY. Now don't be nervous just because you're first to sing, dear.

SOPHIE. Thanks, Mrs D.

(SONG: ***MY LOVE IS HERE TO STAY****)*

*(***SPARKLE*** was planning to sing the same song, so we see the look of horror and disgust on ***SPARKLE****'s face.* ***SOPHIE*** *is doing a great job of this lively song, even doing some little moves, which infuriates* ***SPARKLE*** *even more.* ***SPARKLE*** *looks in her bag and grabs her music file to find another set of sheet music to perform, and chooses something to outdo* ***SOPHIE***. ***SPARKLE****'s repertoire is quite extensive.)*

SOPHIE.

GREY SKIES ARE GONNA SOON BE OVER
THEY'LL SOON BE FAR AWAY
I WILL BE STANDING BY YOUR SHOULDER
MY LOVE IS HERE TO STAY.

MOVE OVER BABY, HERE I COME
SUMMER IS NEARLY HERE
MOVE OVER DARLIN', YOU'RE THE ONE
I WANT TO BE RIGHT NEAR

HONEY YOUR BLUES WILL NOW BE GONE, OH,
I'M WITH YOU DAY BY DAY
WE'LL SOON BE HAPPY GROWING OLDER
MY LOVE IS HERE, MY LOVE IS HERE
MY LOVE IS HERE TO STAY

(Next up is **DANIEL**. *His voice is clearly breaking, and is embarrassed, but perseveres, much to the praise and encouragement of* **MRS DEWBERRY**. **JESS** *and* **CASSIE** *clearly put him down as a 'NO'.)*

(SONG: ***I LIKE TO SING****)*

DANIEL.

WHEN I WAS A LITTLE BOY I OFTEN FELT LIKE QUITE A FOOL
COS I WAS THE ONLY ONE WHO JOINED THE CHOIR IN MY SCHOOL
AND WHEN I TOOK THE STAGE I KNEW I FOUND MY DESTINY
TO BE A FAMOUS SINGER JUST LIKE PAV – A RO – TTI!

I LIKE TO SING... *(goes out of tune)*
I LIKE TO SING... *(goes out of tune)*
I'M GONNA BE A FAMOUS SINGER JUST LIKE PAV – A RO – TTI!

I LIKE TO SING... *(goes out of tune)*
I LIKE TO SING... *(goes out of tune)*
I'M GONNA BE A FAMOUS SINGER JUST LIKE PAV – A RO – TTI!

(Next up is **STEPHANIE**, *who sings* ***'AMAZING GRACE'****.)*

(She hands her music to the pianist, and mumbles some instructions to her. **STEPHANIE** *has a beautiful voice but fumbles over the words, stops and starts, needs to find the lyric sheet, and is giggly with it. Pianist desperately tries to keep up.)*

(SONG: ***AMAZING GRACE****)*

STEPHANIE.

AMAZING GRACE
HOW SWEET THE S.S.S.S... SOUND.
THAT SAVED A WRETCH LIKE...

(forgotten next word)

Sorry... *(tries again – sung)* that saved a wretch... *(spoken)* Oh...what is it? *(looks in her pocket for lyrics. Sings)* ...that saved a wretch...

MRS DEWBERRY. *(interrupts frustratedly)* Like me.

STEPHANIE. Pardon?

MRS DEWBERRY. Like ME?

STEPHANIE. You're not a wretch Mrs Dewberry. A little old, maybe, but not a wretch.

MRS DEWBERRY. *(insulted, and said through gritted teeth)* The WORDS, dear. The words? ...'that saved a wretch like me'...?

STEPHANIE. *(light bulb moment)* OH! I GET IT! *(starts giggling but tries to control herself to continue the song)*

STEPHANIE. *(Sung)*

THAT SAVED A WRETCH... LIKE ME!
I ONCE WAS LOST
BUT NOW AM...

(quickly looks at crumpled lyrics sheet she's pulled out for her jeans)

...FOUND.
WAS BLIND...BUT NOW I SEE.

(A bit embarrassed but giggling to mask it, **STEPHANIE** *sits down.)*

MRS DEWBERRY. *(to* **STEPHANIE***)* Never mind, dear... it happens to the best of us. Well, no it doesn't actual... Best not to choose a famous song if you're going to forget the words. Who have we next?

*(***SPARKLE** *is almost perspiring in desperation to show everyone how she can perform.* **MRS DEWBERRY** *puts her out of her misery.)*

MRS DEWBERRY. All right, Sparkle. Let's hear from you before you burst a blood vessel. What are you going to sing?

SPARKLE. *(As she hands well prepared sheet music to pianist)* I'd like to sing 'Little Bird' by J.A. Carter

*(***SPARKLE** *stands in very powerful and theatrical pose to begin singing and waits for her introduction, whilst giving the pianist a glare. The song is classical in nature and quite pretentious.)*

(SONG: ***LITTLE BIRD****)*

SPARKLE.

THE LITTLE BIRD SINGS HIGH IN THE SKY
HIGH IN THE SKY, SHE FLITS AND FIES.
THE LITTLE BIRD SINGS HIGH IN THE SKY
HIGH IN THE SKY, SHE FLIES.

LA LA LA LA LA, LA LA LA LA LA,
LA LA LA LA LA,... LA LA
LA LA LA LA LA, LA LA LA LA LA... LA LA...
LA LA LA LA LA, LA LA LA LA LA,
LA LA LA LA LA,... LA LA *(big pause for effect)*
LA LA LA LA LA, LA LA LA LA LA... LA LA...

(Small round of applause from the children. Some are very in awe of her, others bemused. **SPARKLE** *can clearly sing very well, and has had obvious training.* **MRS DEWBERRY** *is surprised at the song she has chosen, but tries to be encouraging.)*

MRS DEWBERRY. Lovely, as usual. Very interesting song choice. Mmm! *(to* **JEMIMA***)* You're next, dear.

JEMIMA. I...ah...don't have any music, ...sorry.

MRS DEWBURRY. That's all right, dear, just sing it a capella.

JEMIMA. *(to Pianist)* Can I have a 'D' please?

(Pianist plays the note 'D', followed by a G chord.)

(SONG: ***TELL ME****)*

(Despite not having music, part-way through, the clever pianist busks it and plays a wonderful accompaniment underneath. **JEMIMA** *is simply stunning. No arrogance or difficulty, just a gorgeous tone to her voice, and something lovely about her presence.)*

JEMIMA.

TELL ME
WHEN THE NIGHT HAS GONE
WILL YOU STILL REMEMBER ME?
TELL ME
WHEN THE RAIN STOPS FALLING
WILL YOU STILL REMEMBER ME?
I'M NOT WHAT YOU'D IMAGINE
BUT I'VE GOT SO MUCH TO GIVE
TELL ME
WHEN ALL THIS IS OVER
WILL YOU STILL REMEMBER ME?

*(***JESS, CASSIE** *and* **MRS DEWBERRY** *are all pleasantly surprised.* **SPARKLE** *is worried, but tries not to show it.)*

MRS DEWBERRY. That was truly lovely dear. Now who'd like to go next?

(Fade as eager children put their hands up.)

(Lights back up. Time has passed, and it's obvious everyone in the room has been heard. Everyone is seated on the floor waiting as **JESS, CASSIE** *and* **MRS DEWBERRY** *finish talking amongst themselves.)*

JESS. OK. Thank you for your patience. Can the following people please stand on my left? Courtney Jones,

Stephanie Wilkins, Jonathan Spiers, Daniel Waters, Julia Mason... *(more names depending on the size of the cast)*

Thank you very much for coming today. You have all done a wonderful job. Please take a letter from Cassie on your way out of this door.

(They all exit a bit unsure of what's happening. Once they are gone...)

JESS. Congratulations to the rest of you. You will be going through to the next round. Please go back to the holding area and wait for further instructions. Well done.

(Everyone is excited and some hug each other. They walk back into the holding room. The rejected ones are getting their bags and saying goodbye to the others, and the successful ones are just walking back in when the infamous **SEBASTIAN RICKTER** *enters the room with his entourage.)*

(Everyone stops. **SEBASTIAN** *is tall, confident, wears a cravat, waistcoat, and is carrying a puppy. It's a very quiet, 'pin-dropping' moment. No one dare speaks. As he walks through the crowd of children, it's almost like he's walking through cockroaches. He stops when he comes to* **HUGO**, *who is dressed very similarly, and smiles. Then suddenly drops the smile and waits for the children to move out the way. As he approaches the other side of the room, he whispers to* **JESS**, *points to some of the children, and they are shortly also joining those going home.)*

*(***SPARKLE** *is preening herself in front of him, with the cheesiest of smiles, and trying to catch his eye with cute little waves. He politely acknowledges her, and then whispers to his bodyguards:)*

SEBASTIAN. Make sure that girl's mother is kept a million miles away from me.

(He exits.)

JESS. Right, let's get back to rehearsals. The following numbers please head to Mrs Dewberry's room here on my right. 236, 237, 241, 246, 249, 252...

(Lights fade as children do as they're told.)

(MUSIC: Scene Change)

Scene 5

(The audition day is over. Mass exodus of children leaving the venue. Kids walking home, meeting their parents, etc. We follow **HUGO** *and* **CHARLIE** *as they are heading to the car park where* **MAGGIE** *will be waiting.* **CHARLIE** *is still tossing his tennis ball.)*

CHARLIE. Yeh, I'm going to football practice tonight. *(suddenly)* Why don't you come? It's great fun. You'll love it. Where do you live? Is it far?

HUGO. I live on the corner of Stratton Drive and Dean Street.

CHARLIE. You are KIDDING! I live in Dean Street too! That's incredible! We're gonna be great friends, Hugo. *(put his arm around him)* Great friends.

(looks up) Who is that mad woman waving in this direction? *(he looks behind him as well)*

HUGO. *(slightly embarrassed)* Um...that's my...mum.

CHARLIE. Ask her if you can come to football practice tonight. My dad'll drive you home. It's just down in Pearson's Park.

(They've now reached **HUGO***'s mum)*

CHARLIE. Hello Mrs Finch. I'm Charlie.

MAGGIE. Hello, dear. Hugo, come on, we've got to get back. You know what Tuesday evenings are like when your brother comes for tea.

HUGO. Charlie was wondering if I could go to football practice with him tonight – at Pearson's Park? It's the funniest thing, Mummy, Charlie lives in Dean Street too!

MAGGIE. Oh really? Which side? The respectable side or the common side?

CHARLIE. Didn't know there was such a thing! Number 23 Mrs Finch – has a red door and an unusual cockerel on the roof! My dad won't mind at all dropping Hugo home, Mrs Finch. Hugo's told me he's never played football before! He's such a tease.

*(**MAGGIE** just stares at **CHARLIE**, and then **HUGO**.)*

MAGGIE. Well, he hasn't. Except for that brief moment at Elocution Camp, as punishment. I'm sorry Charles, but Hugo might injure himself, not to mention get dirty. He has cello practice to do and can't afford to damage his fingers if he's going to enter the Charlesford Music Competition next month. Isn't that right, dear?

HUGO. Please, Mummy. *(**HUGO** pulls his mum aside so **CHARLIE** doesn't hear)* I never get invited to anything, or to play with anybody. Please?

*(**MAGGIE** melts a bit seeing **HUGO** so excited about making a friend.)*

MAGGIE. What time will Hugo be back, Charles?

CHARLIE. 8.30 I reckon Mrs Finch.

(Both boys are getting very excited that they might be able to go together.)

MAGGIE. You'll have to do your cello practice when you return Hugo...and NO INJURIES at all, do you hear, or you'll never be allowed out again!

*(**HUGO** hugs his mum. She looks slightly embarrassed about his public affection.)*

HUGO. Thanks Mummy. I'll promise to take care.

MAGGIE. Come on, Charles, I'll drive you home so I can check this is permissible with your father.

*(**HUGO** is so excited he can hardly contain himself! They exit, **CHARLIE** walking behind.)*

CHARLIE. Thanks, Mrs Finch... and the name's Charlie!

(Lights fade.)

(MUSIC: Scene Change)

Scene 6

(Later that evening. Outside **LILY***'s house.* **TOM** *is watering the garden.* **ERIC** *is having his evening walk.)*

ERIC. Evening Tom. Those hyacinths are coming up nicely.

TOM. Evening Eric. Yes they are. Lovely night for a stroll.

ERIC. It is indeed. How are things with you?

TOM. Yeh... OK. Things aren't much different to our last chat to be honest Eric. Laura's really concerned we haven't told the children about the... you know... I just don't want to break their heart. It's not like it's their fault.

ERIC. I know, Tom, but there's never going to be an easy way to tell them. The most important thing is that they feel safe and secure in their parents love. Kids just want a mum and a dad who care about them, are interested in them and show them they are loved on a daily basis. Whether they live under the same roof... or not.

TOM. Does your grandaughter miss her dad?

ERIC. Every day. That's why I won't leave her till the day I die! And that's a long way off if I have anything to do with it!

TOM. She's very lucky to have you.

ERIC. *(pause)* Your kids are too. Enjoy the night.

(**ERIC** *continues down the road and leaves* **TOM** *to think about their conversation.)*

(SONG: ***KEEP THE HEART WITHIN OUR HOME****)*

TOM.

I'VE TRIED TO MAKE A DIFFERENCE

LAURA.

HE'S TRIED TO MAKE A CHANGE

TOM.

SHE'S TRIED TO MAKE THINGS EASIER
BUT IT JUST ENDS UP THE SAME

LAURA.

NEITHER ONE IS GUILTY
WE JUST GOT MARRIED FAR TOO YOUNG

TOM.

NOW WE'VE GOT TO WORK TOGETHER
TO KEEP THE FAMILY ONE

BOTH.

KEEP THE HEART WITHIN OUR HOME
NO MATTER WHERE WE ARE
RESPECT AND LOVE EACH OTHER
EVEN WHEN WE ARE APART
KEEP THE HEART WITHIN OUR HOME
THIS IS MY ONLY DREAM
THAT OUR CHILDREN WILL GROW UP AND KNOW
HOW MUCH THEY MEAN TO ME.

TOM.

NO ONE KNOWS EXACTLY WHAT THEIR LIFE IS ALL ABOUT

LAURA.

WE MAKE THE BEST DECISIONS WHILE WE TRY TO WORK IT OUT

TOM.

NEITHER ONE IS GUILTY

LAURA.

NEITHER ONE TO BLAME

BOTH.

WE'VE GROWN UP WANTING DIFFERENT THINGS
BUT ONE THING THAT REMAINS IS TO
KEEP THE HEART WITHIN OUR HOME
NO MATTER WHERE WE ARE
RESPECT AND LOVE EACH OTHER
EVEN WHEN WE ARE APART
KEEP THE HEART WITHIN OUR HOME
THIS IS MY ONLY DREAM
THAT OUR CHILDREN WILL GROW UP AND KNOW
HOW MUCH THEY MEAN TO ME.

TOM.

THAT MY CHILDREN WILL GROW UP AND KNOW
HOW MUCH THEY MEAN...TO ME.

(Lights fade.)

(MUSIC: Scene Change)

Scene 7

(Day 3 of Auditions. Next morning.)

*(**CHARLIE** and **HUGO** walking to the auditions. We see **HUGO**'s arm in a sling.)*

CHARLIE. So exactly HOW MAD was she? Did my dad manage to smooth things over? I'm really sorry, Hugo. *(**CHARLIE** puts his arm around **HUGO**, but accidentally causes him more pain)*

HUGO. OWW!... Well as you can imagine the 'discussion' about my injury lasted well towards midnight, and Daddy said I didn't have to worry he could fix everything. *(looks confused, doesn't understand)*

*(**CHARLIE** takes **HUGO**'s rucksack and puts it on his back.)*

It really isn't as bad as it looks. I think Mummy's just being over cautious.

CHARLIE. I can't tell you how bad I feel Hugo, really. I thought you'd enjoy it.

HUGO. Enjoy it? I had the BEST TIME EVER!!!! I loved it, Charlie. And being allowed to get all muddy was so much fun! *(we see **HUGO** really alive, more relaxed and less stuffy)* ...And when I kicked that ball into the goal...

*(**CHARLIE** cheers)*

It was INCREDIBLE! Worth every injury! I now know why you love it so much. And how cool to have your dad cheering on the sidelines.

Actually, there were loads of parents there, weren't there? *(just dawns on him)*

CHARLIE. Always is! You were awesome, Hugo. You should join the team. We'll invite your dad next time, yeh?

HUGO. *(not convinced)* ...Yeah.

*(**CHARLIE** puts his arm around **HUGO** again, with another "OWWW" from **HUGO**, followed by them both laughing.)*

(They enter the audition room.)

(Lights fade.)

Scene 8

*(***SEBASTIAN*** and ***RUPERT*** on the golf course, having a recreational business meeting.)*

RUPERT. Don't worry Sebastian. Your investment is safe and secure. Those shares won't be shifting. *(hits golf ball)* So how's the new show coming? My darling Hugo auditioned for it. Have you come across him yet?

SEBASTIAN. I try and sit out of the initial process. Bores me to tears. Can't stand the snivelling when they don't get through – not to mention the parents. Ghastly!

(They briefly look at each other – ***RUPERT*** *worried he's being referred to as a ghastly parent, and* ***SEBASTIAN*** *hoping that* ***RUPERT*** *doesn't become one of those ghastly parents.* ***SEBASTIAN*** *hits the golf ball.)*

SEBASTIAN. I was there briefly yesterday, and I tell you, Rupert, if you want a job done, you have to do it yourself. I walked amongst them, and many of them just looked 'wrong'. Surely my assistants have read my brief. They'll give these darlings false hope if they don't sift them through properly from the start.

RUPERT. So what made you decide to advertise the auditions this time?

SEBASTIAN. I wanted to find someone different. Someone slightly raw with a depth of character that can't be taught, it has to be lived. A lot of the kids I get sent through from agents, who *act* like they're acting. I just want it real. Natural talent. *(hits another ball)* So your boy Hugo. What does he look like?

*(***RUPERT*** takes his wallet out and shows* ***SEBASTIAN*** *a photo of* ***HUGO****.)*

SEBASTIAN. Ah yes – I think I saw him yesterday. Nice clothes.

RUPERT. The trouble is, Sebastian, yesterday he joined another boy he met at the audition and played a game of football for the first time. *(says the word 'football' like* *it's a dirty word)* ...and injured his shoulder. I really hope this won't affect any casting decisions? *(says this hopefully)*

SEBASTIAN. *(hits ball)* Ah yes, I heard about that. I'm sure he'll do fine, Rupert. No need to worry. *(looks at his watch)* Crikey, look at the time. Thanks for the game, Rupert. A lovely idea. Must do it again.

*(**SEBASTIAN** exits. We see **RUPERT** get his mobile out and call his wife.)*

RUPERT. Darling it's me – it's all sort... uh huh... yes, don't worry... Hugo's bound to get the part.

(Lights fade.)

(MUSIC: Scene Change)

Scene 9

(Day 3 – dance auditions)

*(Choreographer (***JACKSON***), walks in exuding confidence and control. Quite a large class of kids. We see some children warming up and stretching, wearing all the right dance gear, including* **SPARKLE** *and* **LILY***. They take their fancy shoes out of proper dance bags, and* **JEMIMA** *is getting her shoes out of a plastic bag. She's wearing her ballet leotard and feels stupid. Other first timers look lost.* **HUGO** *is in the corner of the room giggling every so often reading a Simpson's comic, which he's obviously never read before. Talking to the staff is* **SPARKLE***'s mother –* **LETICIA***.)*

LETICIA. *(over-the-top and very very loud – handing out very posh cupcakes to all the staff)* There's one for each of you. They're from a very exclusive shop on the High Street. I know how exhausting casting must be… *(laughs)*

Anyway, I've got one here for Sebastian. I do know he's quite partial to a French Fancy… But I thought, I'll try something a bit more exotic for a change. *(laughs – then suddenly changes to more serious)* Make sure he gets it, won't you!

(back to over-the-top trying to impress voice) Anyway, must dash, off to that shop to get some focaccia pizza for tea. *(exits the casting room)*

JACKSON. *(to casting assistants)* What's the deal with the boy in the sling?

CASSIE. Sebastian has said he's through this round of auditions.

JACKSON. He hardly looks like a dancer *(we hear more giggling from* **HUGO***)* – or right for this show. Oh well, what Sebastian wants, Sebastian gets. *(claps hands to get attention)* OK, everyone. Let's get going with a warm-up.

JACKSON. OK. Great. Let's learn the routine that goes with the song you learnt yesterday. Let me hear you sing it first. *(to pianist)* Marjorie, can you bring them in, please?

(We hear half of this song just with piano accompaniment first. All the kids sing it, some reluctantly, others over-confidently. It's a bit half-hearted.)

(SONG: ***GOTTA GIVE IN TO THE MUSIC*** *(Short Version))*

COMPANY.

FEEL THE RHYTHM OF THE MUSIC
MAKES YOU WANNA DANCE
WHEN THE BEAT GETS IN YOUR FEET THEN
YOU DON'T STAND A CHANCE
YOU GOTTA
SWAY YOUR HIPS AND MOVE YOUR FINGERS
TURN YOUR BODY ROUND
LOOSEN UP A LITTLE BABY
WHEN YOU HEAR THIS SOUND

COME AND FEEL THE RHYTHM EVERYWHERE
OH YEAH
WHEN YOU'RE FLYING HIGH YOU'RE NEARLY THERE...
WO OH YOU

GOTTA GIVE IN TO THE MUSIC OF THE RHYTHM OF YOUR SOUL
YOU GOTTA GIVE IN TO THE MUSIC AND LET IT TAKE CONTROL
AND TAKE YOU, TAKE YOU TO YOUR DREAM, AHA
TAKE YOU, TAKE YOU TO YOUR DREAM.

JACKSON. Great. But it will need to be bigger than that, guys. Here's the routine. Watch me first.

5, 6, 7, 8...

(MUSIC: ***GOTTA GIVE IN TO THE MUSIC*** *(Dance Version 1))*

(**JACKSON** *does the routine that blows the kids away. Some of them mini-marking it and trying to learn it as he goes, most just left with their mouths open.)*

JACKSON. OK. Here we go. Your turn.

5, 6, 7, 8…

(MUSIC: ***GOTTA GIVE IN TO THE MUSIC*** *(Dance Version 2))*

(**JACKSON** *takes them through the first 16 bars of the routine. We can see those who can clearly do it, and those who have no rhythm at all. Casting assistants are madly writing notes and talking amongst themselves. We see* **JESS** *get up and walk around to encourage them not to give up.)*

JACKSON. Right. Now... Let's see you four at a time. Get into positions please.

(They all scurry to keep up, and line up uncomfortably in rows of four. **SPARKLE** *is in the first line.)*

(MUSIC: ***GOTTA GIVE IN TO THE MUSIC*** *(Dance Version 3))*

(Piano accompaniment is played, and we see the first group do well. **SPARKLE** *can do it all.)*

(The other groups do the routine. We see **JEMIMA** *is just keeping up,* **CHARLIE** *has a bit of difficulty but decides to throw himself into it.* **LILY** *does really well but looks tired.)*

JACKSON. Excellent, well done, all of you. Let's take a quick loo break before we learn the next bit. We'll also be looking for a small group of you to do a tap routine. Who can tap?

(Several put their hands up. **SPARKLE***'s arm is the highest and she makes sure everyone can see her.)*

JACKSON. Great. Can you get your shoes on and I'll quickly teach you the routine while the others have a break.

(Some kids leave the room. The tap kids quickly put their shoes on. **JACKSON** *talks to casting assistants.* **CHARLIE** *heads over to where* **HUGO** *is sitting.)*

HUGO. Charlie, this is BRILLIANT! *(referring to his comic)* This Homer Simpson guy is the most ludicrous father on the planet! The result of too many donuts I think you'll find! And look – apparently, it says on the back page, that they've even made a movie about him! Can you believe it!

CHARLIE. Mate, you gotta get out more!

JACKSON. OK you guys! *(gathering the tap dancers together)* Here's the routine, watch me first.

(MUSIC: Tap Number)

*(***JACKSON** *bursts into an incredibly difficult tap routine, wowing them all again.)*

(MUSIC: Tap Number (Reprise))

(The tap kids then do the same routine, almost perfectly. **SPARKLE** *and* **LILY** *almost eyeing each other to see who is better, both doing really well.)*

*(***JEMIMA** *is stunned. When the routine is over,* **JACKSON** *talks with the casting assistants about the tap kids.* **SPARKLE** *is full of smiles right in front of them.* **LILY** *heads over to her to take her shoes off.)*

JEMIMA. I can't believe what I just saw! Lily you are incredible, you're all there with arms, head... *(demonstrates)* everything!

LILY. *(sighing and catching her breath, sits next to* **JEMIMA** *on the floor)* I'm SHATTERED! *(smiling)* I haven't done a tap routine for a month. Do you think they could tell? Hope not. That 'step ball change shuffle pickup wing drop' almost caught me out! *(notices* **JEMIMA***'s looking quite faint)* Sorry...you ok?

JEMIMA. I feel sick, Lily. What am I doing here? I can't do any of this. He showed you the routine ONCE. And you could just do it. I'm better off going now. *(starts to get up)*

LILY. *(firmly)* Now you listen to me, Jemima: being able to tap is NOT a requirement for the main role. Remember that. I'm pleased I've got another chance to be in the show, and Mum and Dad's tap fees weren't in vain! I don't think I've got a shot at the lead, Jem, but YOU do. You're really different. I'm just the same as everyone else. Honestly.

JACKSON. *(claps hands)* OK. Let's get back to the main routine, everyone? Let's take it from the top please.

5, 6, 7, 8...

(Fade to black while they're dancing.)

(Then Lights up and we see the routine fully learnt, all singing and dancing, like a finale number.)

(SONG: ***FEEL THE RHYTHM****)*

ALL.

FEEL THE RHYTHM OF THE MUSIC
MAKES YOU WANNA DANCE
WHEN THE BEAT GETS IN YOUR FEET THEN
YOU DON'T STAND A CHANCE
YOU GOTTA
SWAY YOUR HIPS AND MOVE YOUR FINGERS
TURN YOUR BODY ROUND
LOOSEN UP A LITTLE BABY
WHEN YOU HEAR THIS SOUND

COME AND FEEL THE RHYTHM EVERYWHERE
OH YEAH
WHEN YOU'RE FLYING HIGH YOU'RE NEARLY THERE...
WO OH YOU

GOTTA GIVE IN TO THE MUSIC OF THE RHYTHM OF YOUR SOUL
YOU GOTTA GIVE IN TO THE MUSIC AND LET IT TAKE CONTROL
AND TAKE YOU, TAKE YOU TO YOUR DREAM...UH HUH.

TAKE YOU, TAKE YOU TO YOUR DREAM.

KEEP YOURSELF TOGETHER WHILE YOU
TRY TO LET IT GO – NO OH
YOU'VE GOT TO SURRENDER
IF YOU WANT THE GROOVE TO FLOW
CLOSE YOUR EYES AND HEAR THE BEAT
TIL YOU JUST GO INSANE
WHEN YOU'RE BREATHING MUSIC YOU CAN
NEVER BE THE SAME

COME AND FEEL THE RHYTHM EVERYWHERE
OH YEAH
WHEN YOU'RE FLYING HIGH YOU'RE NEARLY THERE...
WO OH YOU

GOTTA GIVE IN TO THE MUSIC OF THE RHYTHM OF YOUR SOUL
YOU GOTTA GIVE IN TO THE MUSIC AND LET IT TAKE CONTROL
AND TAKE YOU, TAKE YOU TO YOUR DREAM...UH HUH.
TAKE YOU, TAKE YOU TO YOUR DREAM.
TAKE YOU, TAKE YOU TO YOUR DREAM.
AND TAKE YOU, TAKE YOU TO YOUR DREAM.

(As the last line of the song is repeated we see the kids collecting their bags and leaving the casting room into the streets to go home.)

(Scene change into **LILY***'s house.)*

Scene 10

*(**LILY** and **JEMIMA** arrive at **LILY**'s house after the audition.)*

LILY. Hi, Mum. This is Jemima. She's auditioning for the show also.

LAURA. Hi Jemima. Lovely to meet you. How did today go?

*(**LAURA** gets drinks and food for the girls.)*

LILY. Yeh, really good. I got a chance to TAP today!! I was so excited 'cos they're also looking for kids who can tap for a special number. I think I've got a real chance, Mum.

LAURA. That's great, honey. But don't give up on getting the main part, darling. You are very talented.

JEMIMA. That's what I tell her!

LAURA. So where are you from Jemima? Travelled a long way?

JEMIMA. No, Mrs Jackson. I live down the road in no 142!

LILY. Yeh, Mum, can you believe it? We're practically neighbours!

LAURA. How funny! Which theatre school do you go to Jemima?

JEMIMA. None actually. This is my first ever audition. Don't know how I've got this far really.

LILY. Pure talent Jem. Stop being so shy. You're a natural!

*(**TOM** arrives home from work and enters the kitchen.)*

TOM. Hello!

LILY. Hi, Dad!

TOM. *(cheery)* Who's this then?

LILY. This is my new friend Jemima. She lives at number 142! Can you believe it!

TOM. You wouldn't be Eric's granddaughter, by any chance would you?

JEMIMA. *(surprised)* Yes...actually. Do you know him?

TOM. Just to say hello to when he goes for his evening walk. He talks about his "precious Jemima" all the time. How is he?

JEMIMA. Fine, thank you.

LILY. Anyway, we're just gonna go and practise the routine for tomorrow so we knock Sparkle off her pedestal!! HA!

*(**LILY** grabs **JEMIMA** and runs upstairs.)*

JEMIMA. *(on her way up)* Nice to meet you!

(Once they've gone...)

TOM. Lily is buzzing. Did her audition go well today?

LAURA. Seems to. She got to show off her tap skills, so she's happy... For now.

TOM. What's that meant to mean Laura?

LAURA. I'm scared, Tom. I'm really worried about Lily and the boys. The divorce is going to hit them like a tonne of bricks. There'll be no warning, no signs.

TOM. *(interrupts)* It's just one of those things, Lor, two people growing apart, wanting different things.

LAURA. They're too young to really understand that Tom.

TOM. *(pause)* We've agreed to make it as painless as possible, you know that. There just never seems a good time to tell the kids.

*(**LILY** interrupts, coming into the kitchen to get another drink, still in a good mood.)*

LILY. Tell the kids what?

*(Freeze with **TOM** and **LAURA** looking at each other.)*

(Snap black out – end of Act One.)

ACT TWO

*(SONG: **LIFE IS WHAT YOU MAKE IT**)*

(Next day. All final kids on stage. We see another song and dance routine taking shape.)

COMPANY.

LIFE IS WHAT YOU MAKE IT,
SO LET'S MAKE IT FUN,
PUSH THOSE CLOUDS AWAY, HEY HEY,
TODAY'S YOUR DAY.

AND I'M TELLING YOU THAT
LIFE IS WHAT YOU MAKE IT,
SO LET'S MAKE IT SHINE,
YOU CAN MAKE YOUR WAY, HEY HEY,
TODAY'S EVERYTHING YOU WANT IT TO BE.

WOAH
OOH

NO-ONE KNOWS WHAT THE FUTURE HOLDS,
EVERY DAY IS DIFFERENT,
THAT'S THE FUN ABOUT IT!
AS YOUR LIFE SLOWLY EVOLVES,
MAKE EACH DAY COUNT,
JUMP UP AND SHOUT,
YOU MUST REMEMBER!

LIFE IS WHAT YOU MAKE IT,
SO LET'S MAKE IT FUN,
PUSH THOSE CLOUDS AWAY, HEY HEY,
TODAY'S YOUR DAY,

AND I'M TELLING YOU THAT
LIFE IS WHAT YOU MAKE IT,
SO LET'S MAKE IT FUN,

PUSH THOSE CLOUDS AWAY, HEY HEY,
TODAY'S YOUR DAY,

AND I'M TELLING YOU THAT
LIFE IS WHAT YOU MAKE IT,
SO LET'S MAKE IT SHINE,
YOU CAN MAKE A WAY, HEY HEY,
TODAY'S EVERYTHING YOU WANT IT TO BE.

WOAH
OOH
WOAH
YEAH! YEAH!

JACKSON. Great. That's a wrap. Well done, everyone.

(Everyone applauds)

JESS. That's lunch everyone. 30 mins please.

*(**LETICIA**'s head appears through the door (or at a glass window) to bring **SPARKLE** her smoked salmon and cream cheese bagels, freshly squeezed orange juice, and humidifier for clear vocal passageways. Her lunch is delivered in an extravagant picnic hamper. No other parent is allowed to be here. **LETICIA** can't see the harm in just popping up to deliver her daughter some lunch. Really she wants to be nosey.)*

*(**SPARKLE** is sitting on her own.)*

*(As **LETICIA** enters, the casting assistants, **JESS** and **CASSIE**, are furious she's up to her old tricks.)*

LETICIA. Cassie, darling! *(air kisses)* So wonderful to see you again. You too, Jessica. How's the career? *(to **CASSIE**)* I saw you on that soap, what was it called? – you were wonderful, darling – deserved a much better part, with your blue eyes and fabulous bone structure.

CASSIE. *(politely)* Why thank you, Mrs Moon.

LETICIA. Call me Leticia darling! So tell me, is there anyone here as vibrant and as talented as my Sparkle?

JESS. *(firmly)* You know parents are not permitted to be here, Mrs Moon.

LETICIA. *(Diva-ish)* Is a mother not entitled to bring her only child some food if she's left her lunch at home??

(We all see **SPARKLE** *clearly take out a lunch box and flask out of her bag.* **LETICIA** *tries to distract them with her catchphrase...)*

LETICIA. "Sparkle by day, Sparkle by night, Sparkle Moon is an audience's delight!" Ha ha ha ha... no seriously, *(slightly worried)* is there anyone as talented as my wonder child? *(takes* **CASSIE** *aside)* She's born for this, Cassie, I'm sure you can see it because you're in the business – you know talent when you see it.

*(***JESS** *is rolling her eyes behind them.)*

Has Sebastian seen Sparkle's updated CV?

JESS. *(interrupting)* Sebastian has all the CVs, Mrs Moon, I handed them to him myself.

LETICIA. *(grabs another CV out of her handbag)* Here, darling, *(to* **CASSIE***)* make sure he gets it, won't you, precious? *(places a £20 note in her hand and winks)*

*(***CASSIE** *and* **JESS** *look at each other rolling their eyes and* **JESS** *takes the picnic hamper to* **SPARKLE**. **LETICIA***, who is meant to be on her way out, spots* **MRS DEWBERRY** *in the corner of the room.)*

LETICIA. YOO HOO!! Mrs Dewberry... It's me! Leticia Moon... Sparkle's mother?... Mrs Dewberry?...

(We see **MRS DEWBERRY** *look down her nose through her glasses wishing she hadn't been spotted and trying to exit quickly.)*

(Lights fade.)

Scene 2

(After lunch. Acting auditions: duologues and cold reading.)

(Scene opens with **CASSIE** *and* **JESS** *checking registers and pairs of children.* **JEMIMA** *is with a nice girl called Mia.* **HUGO** *with* **OSCAR**, **CHARLIE** *with* **JESSE**, **SPARKLE** *with* **LILY**. **LILY** *isn't quite herself. She looks tired and worried. Everyone is realising this is it: crunch time. Everyone deals with their nerves in different ways, but tension is high.)*

JESS. Right, hi everyone. Hope you enjoyed your lunch break, and hopefully you've had a rehearsal with the acting partner we assigned you earlier.

(We see **SPARKLE** *having a bit of an issue with* **LILY**, *and* **LILY** *just firmly shrugging* **SPARKLE** *off.)*

(People settle in, put their bags down, get their scripts out etc.)

HUGO. Nervous about the acting session, Charlie?

CHARLIE. Not now, Hugo. Your tips on memorising lines was awesome! I'd normally be freaking out having to read something. Lucky we had a couple of days to learn this stuff. Thanks man.

JESS. OK. Jesse and Edward, you're up first.

HUGO. Good luck, Charlie!

CHARLIE. I think you're meant to say "Break a leg!" *(laughs)*

*(***JESSE** *&* **EDWARD** *move into position to perform duologue.)*

EDWARD. Happy birthday to you... Happy birthday to you...

JESSE. *(interrupts)* SHHHH!! QUIET!! No one's meant to know it's my birthday.

EDWARD. Why? I love birthdays! I'd have 'em every day if I could!

JESSE. *(loud whisper)* They're meant to think I'm younger than I really am... *(looks around to make sure no one has been listening)*

EDWARD. Who are?

JESSE. The government. *(looking oddly around as if there are spies)* They have spies everywhere. *(looks behind* **EDWARD** *'s ear)*

EDWARD. Hey! *(brushing him away)* But I don't get it?! When you get older you can drink, watch movies your mum said you couldn't before, not to mention Playstation games that are practically banned, get a job, earn some money, drive a car! You become "responsible".

JESSE. But that's just it. I don't WANT to be responsible, I want to have fun and do stupid things... I like building, drawing, watching shows with my kid brother... *(almost whispering)* ... I even went to Disneyland last week and loved it... Look, I'm still not too big *(measures his height with his hand)* to get into the 'It's a Small World' ride!...

EDWARD. Well, ...whatever you say...if that's the way you want to play it, your secret's safe with me – but they're gonna find out your age at some point.

You'll be growing facial hair soon!!

JESSE. Very funny... Quick!! – someone's coming... one, two, three *(they do paper, rock scissors trying to be 'normal')*

(Lights fade.)

(Lights up. We see that **LILY** *and* **SPARKLE** *have just finished their duologue.)*

JESS. Thanks everyone. Take five while we talk amongst ourselves.

*(***JESS** *and other casting assistants discuss who they want to see again.)*

(In a corner of the room...)

SPARKLE. What the hell do you think you're doing, Lily? Are you trying to jeopardise my chances, just because you don't have a chance in hell? You're so selfish.

LILY. Leave it, Sparkle. *(She's looking for something in her bag)*

SPARKLE. This is my CAREER we're talking about. You know how important the acting audition is. It's like you weren't even here. I want this role more than anything in the world... You even mumbled the words! How am I meant to act against THAT?

LILY. *(fights back)* Why does everything have to be about you? I've had a hell of a night. My world has fallen apart, but I'm still here Sparkle. I didn't let you down.

SPARKLE. *(sarcastically)* Oh really?

LILY. It's none of your business, why can't you back off? I've not slept a wink last night *(turns to Sparkle and looks her directly in the face)* after being told that my parents – my perfectly loving parents – are getting divorced. And I knew NOTHING about it. Nothing. *(to herself)* I still can't believe it. I thought I had the perfect family. I thought they were happy. *(**LILY** is almost in a daze)* I was sure they were happy. *(directing this to **JEMIMA**, who has been listening to all of this)* Didn't you think they were happy, Jem?

*(**JEMIMA** hugs **LILY**. **SPARKLE** feels bad.)*

*(The scene is interrupted by **CASSIE**.)*

CASSIE. OK. Can I have your attention, please? Can the following people please come forward to collect another small passage of script. Charlie, Edward, Jemima, Mia, Oscar, and... *(looks through notes for suspense)* ...Sparkle.

*(Each one of them comes up and collects the paper from another assistant. **SPARKLE** is relieved and offers a look of smugness to **LILY**.)*

CHARLIE. So we learn this for tomorrow?

CASSIE. No we'll do it now. Cold reading.

*(No one else is bothered, but **CHARLIE** instantly goes cold. He stares at the page but can hardly move. **HUGO**, who has been watching this, suddenly shrieks with pain in his shoulder.)*

HUGO. OWWWW...AWWWW... Charlie, can you help me? Can you call my mum?

CASSIE. *(annoyed)* What's going on?

HUGO. *(to casting assistants)* Sorry – can Charlie just give me a hand while someone else goes first? OWW...

(Casting assistants aren't fussed.)

JESS. Ok. Edward, we'll start with you.

*(***CHARLIE*** and ***HUGO*** head out into the corridor. ***CHARLIE***, who believes that ***HUGO*** is in a huge amount of pain is shocked to see ***HUGO*** suddenly stop the pain noises.)*

HUGO. Right Charlie, give me the script.

CHARLIE. WHAT? Huh? I don't get it? *(he's really puzzled)*

HUGO. You froze in there. There is no way you'll get through this audition when they hear you read cold. And I think you've got a real chance Charlie, I really do.

Right. Sit here. I'll read it out. You repeat it. Remember to get pictures and sounds in your head. I reckon we've got 10 minutes. Let's go.

CHARLIE. *(pats* **HUGO** *on the back)* Thanks, man.

HUGO. Watch the shoulder!

(They smile at each other. **CHARLIE** *sits down, closes his eyes, and* **HUGO** *starts to read the monologue.)*

HUGO. I can't tell you why I did it. I've no idea...

(Lights fade.)

(Fade up to the acting audition room, and we catch the end of another boy finishing his monologue. It's very heightened, intense, moving.)

OSCAR. *(intense)* ...forty-five minutes you've had me standing here Stanley. Forty-five bleedin' minutes. Where have you been?... and I'm not having your crappy excuses again. It's freezing. I'm cold and I'm ANGRY.

That's right. I'm ANGRY. I'm sick of you taking advantage. I'm your *brother,* but not your doormat. I'm sick and tired of you treating me like one.

So why, Stanley? Tell me the truth. Why are you late THIS time?

(There's a few seconds' silence and then applause from the other kids.)

JESS. OK. Charlie Harris please. Is Charlie back in the room now?

CHARLIE. Yes, hi... I'm here.

JESS. Great. When you're ready.

*(**CHARLIE** looks at **HUGO**. Looks on the floor, puts his hands behind his back, takes a deep breath and begins his monologue.)*

CHARLIE. I can't tell you why I did it. I've no idea. I'm not going to pretend I know. And I'm not going to blame the voices in my head – which I could do if I chose to... no, it's just a simple mistake. A wrong choice.

We all have choices, don't we?... I mean right now, you can choose to believe me, or not...right? All I can tell you from the bottom of my heart, is...that I didn't mean to do it. It just happened. Faster than I was able to stop it. And by then it was too late.

I didn't mean to do it, Officer. I didn't mean to hurt her...or to leave her there to suffer...all on her...own... *(end)*

*(The room is still after **CHARLIE** speaks. Everyone is moved by the emotion of it. You see the Casting assistants whispering to each other. Out of the shadows you hear a single clap. Followed by another one...and another one. It's **SEBASTIAN**, who had been observing the whole thing, without being seen. He suddenly appears. He has an incredible presence about him.)*

SEBASTIAN. That's the kind of emotion and dedication of character I'm looking for. All of you... *(looks around)*

Did you *feel* that? It moved me. The character of Jonah is a troubled soul and the audience needs to *feel* and worry for him. (**SEBASTIAN** *is teaching them all as he speaks)*

(to **CHARLIE**) Good job. Charlie, is it? (**SEBASTIAN** *shakes his hand)* That's a wrap for today. Final day tomorrow. All of you get some sleep.

(**SEBASTIAN** *goes to whisper something to the Casting Assistants.* **CASSIE** *hands out more paper to the remaining kids, and* **JESS** *goes towards* **HUGO**.)

JESS. Hi Hugo. Mr Rickter would like to see you in his office before you go home, if that's ok? (**HUGO** *is really worried)* Don't worry, honestly. I'll show you where it is.

CHARLIE. I'll wait for you here, Hugo.

(Audition kids pack up and go home, some congratulate **OSCAR** *and* **CHARLIE** *on their good performances.* **HUGO** *and* **JESS** *exit stage right.)*

(**CHARLIE** *gets comfortable and calls his dad on his mobile to tell him the good news of the day.)*

CHARLIE. Hey, Dad? You'll never guess what happened! Sebastian Rickter actually liked me! ... yeh... uh huh...

(MUSIC: Scene Change)

Scene 3

(In **SEBASTIAN***'s office.* **SEBASTIAN** *is sitting comfortably behind his desk.* **HUGO** *enters.)*

SEBASTIAN. Hello, Hugo. *(Stands and puts his hand out to shake)* Don't worry, you're not in trouble. Take a seat.

*(***HUGO** *slowly sits down, nervous.)*

SEBASTIAN. Tell me, Hugo, why do you think Charlie did so well in his audition just now?

HUGO. He's talented, sir. Has an "inner charm" some might say. He even surprised me!

SEBASTIAN. It wouldn't have anything to do with you coaching him in the corridor beforehand, would it?

HUGO. *(surprised)* No, sir, um... I was just helping him learn his lines. That's all. The rest came from Sam. I wouldn't know how to tell him to perform. This is all new to me.

SEBASTIAN. What brought you to these auditions, Hugo?

HUGO. My mother and father thought it might be a good idea for me. They are huge lovers of the arts.

SEBASTIAN. I see. And how did you injure your arm?

HUGO. Football, sir.

SEBASTIAN. Are you good at it?

HUGO. I've never played it before! Charlie invited me to a practice match. It was great fun! I even scored a goal! *(***HUGO***'s face comes alive when he talks about football)*

SEBASTIAN. What do you enjoy more, Hugo? This acting business or football?

HUGO. *(not wanting to insult him)* Oh... I'm not sure, sir. I'm new to both. But... *(hesitant)* ...if I had to choose one, ...to be honest, football makes me feel different.

SEBASTIAN. Different?

HUGO. I suppose I mean... 'free'.

SEBASTIAN. I understand. That's how performing makes *me* feel. And your parents? What do they want you to do?

HUGO. Wear funny suits and be arty farty! *(suddenly realises he's insulting* **SEBASTIAN***'s dress sense and quickly backtracks)*... Oh, sorry... I mean...

SEBASTIAN. *(laughs)* It's OK. Tell me more about your parents.

HUGO. My father is a bit like Frasier, you know that guy from the TV show. Knows a lot about wine, the stock market, plays golf, likes art galleries... My mother seems stressed all the time, but that might be down to looking after my brother.

SEBASTIAN. *(interrupts)* Your brother? I didn't know you had a brother.

HUGO. Not many people do know. His name is William. He's much older than me. He has Down's Syndrome. *(says very matter of fact)* He's loads of fun, has his own flat and has a job. He's great. But Mummy worries about him a lot.

(Although **HUGO** *has no idea* **SEBASTIAN** *is a personal friend of his dad,* **SEBASTIAN***'s eyes have been opened to understanding their family more, and this is evident in his face and body language.)*

HUGO. But she's also busy choosing what clothes I wear, taking me from cello to flute lessons, not to mention extra French and Spanish after school!

SEBASTIAN. But not football?

HUGO. No, sir.

*(***SEBASTIAN** *gets up and gets closer to* **HUGO***, sitting on the edge of his desk.)*

SEBASTIAN. Hugo, between you and me, and from what I've seen of your auditions so far, I'm not quite sure if this business is for you. When you talk about football, you become passionate. *(seriously)* You should always follow passion. Whether you're good at football or not, it is something you need to investigate, spend some time exploring. You need to discover who *you* are. Not who you're expected to be. Do you understand?

HUGO. Yes, sir.

SEBASTIAN. *(stands up)* It's been lovely talking to you, Hugo. I wish you every success with your football. Maybe we'll run into each other again sometime. *(shakes* **HUGO***'s hand)*

HUGO. Thank you, sir.

*(***HUGO*** leaves and* **SEBASTIAN** *is deep in thought.)*

(SONG: ***DREAMS CAN COME TRUE****)*

*(***HUGO*** now in spotlight, all other lights dimmed.)*

HUGO.

MAYBE I CAN DO IT
MAYBE I CAN FIND
SOMETHING I AM GOOD AT
SOMETHING THAT CAN HELP ME FLY

(Spotlight fades up on **JEMIMA**, **HUGO** *freezes.)*

JEMIMA.

TELL ME
WHEN ALL OF THIS IS OVER
WILL YOU STILL REMEMBER ME?

HUGO.

HELP ME FLY

JEMIMA.

TELL ME
WHEN ALL OF THIS IS OVER
WILL YOU STILL REMEMBER ME?

HUGO.

HELP ME FLY

(Spotlight fades up on **LILY** *and remain on* **HUGO** *and* **JEMIMA**.*)*

LILY.

I DON'T KNOW WHERE THIS IS LEADING
I NEVER FELT SO ALONE
THIS ISN'T THE LIFE I BELIEVED IN
SOMEBODY TELL ME WHERE,
WHERE IS MY HOME?

(Spotlight fades up on **SEBASTIAN**. *All four lead characters remain lit.)*

SEBASTIAN.

DREAMS CAN COME TRUE ANY DAY
DREAMS CAN COME TRUE ANYWHERE
JUST HOLD ON TIGHT AND BE READY TO FLY
ANYWHERE, YOUR DREAMS WILL TAKE YOU

(Spotlights fade and company is lit as if in dream state.)

COMPANY.

DREAMS CAN COME TRUE ANY DAY
DREAMS CAN COME TRUE ANYWHERE
JUST HOLD ON TIGHT AND BE READY TO FLY
ANYWHERE, YOUR DREAMS WILL TAKE YOU

DREAMS CAN COME TRUE ANY TIME
DREAMS ONLY NEED AN OPEN MIND
WHAT IS LIFE, WITHOUT A DREAM TO DREAM?

YOUNG OR OLD
RICH OR POOR
THERE'S A DREAM INSIDE YOU
LET IT FLY FAR AND WIDE
AND ONE DAY, YOUR DREAM WILL FIND YOU...

DREAMS CAN COME TRUE ANY DAY
DREAMS CAN COME TRUE ANYWHERE
JUST HOLD ON TIGHT AND BE READY TO FLY
ANYWHERE, YOUR DREAMS WILL TAKE YOU

DREAMS CAN COME TRUE ANY TIME
DREAMS ONLY NEED AN OPEN MIND
WHAT IS LIFE WITHOUT A DREAM TO DREAM?

(We see **HUGO** *sneaking out of his house at night, to attend football practice.)*

HUGO.

WHAT IS LIFE, WITHOUT A DREAM TO DREAM.

(Lights fade.)

(MUSIC: Scene Change)

Scene 4

(Next day – final audition day. **HUGO***'s house.* **HUGO** *has slept in. He's been out all night playing football, without his parents permission.)*

MAGGIE. *(yelling up the stairs)* HUGO! You'll be late for your audition. It's the final day!

*(***HUGO** *enters in his pyjamas.)*

MAGGIE. *(in a panic, raising the pitch of her voice)* What are you doing?! Run upstairs this instance and get washed. If we hurry we'll just make it. *(Looking at watch and madly making a packed lunch and stuffing things in a rucksack)*

HUGO. I didn't get through to the next round.

MAGGIE. What?!

RUPERT. I'll fix it, honey, don't you worry.

*(***RUPERT** *takes his mobile out and starts dialing* **SEBASTIAN***'s private number.)*

HUGO. *(grabs his dad's mobile)* No, Daddy. It's OK. I don't want to do it anymore.

*(***RUPERT** *&* **MAGGIE** *look at each other shocked.)*

MAGGIE. Hugo...

HUGO. *(interrupting)* Mum... it isn't for me. It was great experience, and I loved learning new songs and dance routines, and especially meeting new friends like Charlie.

MAGGIE. Is this his fault? *(to* **RUPERT***)* I knew he'd be a bad influence – he lives down the 'other' end of the street.

HUGO. Mummy! Don't be so ridiculous. But Charlie did introduce me to football – and I really LOVE IT! It's fantastic running through the fresh air with your heart racing, and your blood pumping, and being chased by a bunch of boys much bigger than you! – there's nothing like it.

(**MAGGIE** *&* **RUPERT** *look at their child as if he's adopted! They just don't understand it.)*

HUGO. It's what I want to do. Please, Mum and Dad. Please? I was invited to join the under 12's local team last night.

(**HUGO***'s eyes pop out of his head as he realises he's slipped up.)*

MAGGIE. Last night? HUGO!! You said you wanted to get an early night. I am very disappointed in you Hugo Maximillian Finch. *(turns to hug* **RUPERT***)*

RUPERT. Son, you should never lie to your mother. Look at her.

HUGO. I'm sorry, Mum. *(feels really bad. He's never rebelled against his parents)*

(After and awkward silence...)

RUPERT. Is this what you want, Hugo? To play football?

HUGO. Dad, YES! I love it – and guess what? Most of the dads stand on the sideline yelling things at their kids – you'd enjoy it, Mum *(gives her a cheeky smile)* ...and William can come too.

Maybe you could try it sometime, Dad? (**HUGO** *holds his dad's hand)* We can go together, I'll invite Charlie and his dad around. He can tell you all about it. *(pause)* Dad?

RUPERT. Maggie? *(looking at his wife)*

MAGGIE. *(waits a few seconds, then says very sternly...)* As long as your school work and cello practice doesn't suffer. I only want you to be happy. *(she walks towards* **HUGO** *to hug him. He hugs her back)*

HUGO. Thanks, Mum.

(Lights fade.)

(MUSIC: Scene Change)

Scene 5

(As everyone from the final workshop days all gather, walking from their home, getting off buses, **CHARLIE** *walks down the road, meets* **LILY** *coming out of her front door, then we see* **LILY** *knocking on* **JEMIMA***'s door, the three of them singing and dancing down the road, all really happy.)*

(We see **SPARKLE***'s mother personally delivering a freshly baked cake to the casting assistants, and making a big fuss. As the music finishes, they're about to go into the audition room.)*

JEMIMA. How's everything, Lily? *(in serious tone, really about the divorce)*

LILY. I think it's going to be OK. We had a really long chat last night, and Dad's moving really close by... and we'll see him practically every day, so not much will change. I suppose I'm one of the lucky ones.

*(***SPARKLE** *walks up behind* **LILY** *and* **JEMIMA***.)*

SPARKLE. Lily? ... *(hesitant)* Can I have a word?

*(***JEMIMA** *moves out the way, but not too far.)*

SPARKLE. I just wanted to apologise for how I spoke to you yesterday. I didn't realise what you were going through, and even if I did, I shouldn't have given you an ear-bashing. Will you forgive me?

LILY. Of course. *(hugs)* And I'm sorry if my 'not all with it' performance ruined yours. I hope it didn't.

SPARKLE. Let's face it, those casting directors should know what I'm capable of now. They've seen me enough times!

(They both laugh.)

LILY. Break a leg today, Sparkle.

SPARKLE. *(surprise at* **LILY***'s genuineness)* Thanks Lily. You too.

(They enter the audition room.)

Scene 6

(Inside the audition room we see **SEBASTIAN RICKTER** *sitting in the middle of the casting tables.* **MRS DEWBERRY, JACKSON,** *possibly a producer, also sit behind the tables.* **CASSIE** *&* **JESS** *are standing with their clipboards ready.)*

(An assistant has walked in with the teas and coffees on a tray. Hands a takeaway Costa Coffee to **SEBASTIAN** *first. Then distributes the others...)*

MRS DEWBERRY. Thank you, dear. Nothing like a cup of tea. No sugar thank you.

JACKSON. Cheers. *(take his coffee adds lots of sugar)*

SEBASTIAN. WHO ORDERED THIS? Where is she? How do you expect me to be able to do my job without the correct number of espresso shots I specifically ordered?

*(***CASSIE** *steps in, apologises on behalf of the new girl, writes down the specific order and passes to her and tells her to RUN!)*

*(***CASSIE** *goes to take the wrong coffee from* **SEBASTIAN***...)*

SEBASTIAN. This will do for now... *(hugs the coffee)*

JESS. OK. Can I have your attention please? Firstly, we would like to say a huge thank you to all of you for your hard work, focus and adaptability this week. You have been a terrific bunch of kids to work with.

(Everyone claps.)

JESS. But, as you know we are casting just 2 roles – the role of Jonah, and the role of Stephanie. We've seen you dance, act, and sing, and now we'd like to see you perform the opening number of the show, 3 of you at a time.

So if you could organise yourselves, and we'll get underway.

*(***SPARKLE, LILY** *and* **JEMIMA** *choose to go together.)*

*(SONG: **TOMORROW, TODAY**)*

JEMIMA.

WE'VE BEEN CHASING RAINBOWS,
COS WE'RE TOLD THAT'S WHERE WE'LL FIND.
THE POT OF GOLD THAT HOLDS THE DREAMS WE DREAM.

LILY.

THOUGH DIFFERENT ROADS WE'RE TAKING,
WE'VE GOT TO FOLLOW EVERY SIGN.
AND GIVE OURSELVES THE FREEDOM TO ACHIEVE.

SPARKLE.

THERE MAY BE THINGS TO CHANGE,
THERE MAY BE HILLS TO CLIMB.
BUT WE'LL NEVER REACH OUR DREAMS IF WE DON'T TRY.

ALL 3 GIRLS.

TOMORROW'S ALL WE NEED FOR ANOTHER CHANCE TO DREAM.
DISCOVER POSSIBILITIES WE NEVER KNEW.
TOMORROW'S ALL WE NEED, SO HOLD ON AND BELIEVE.
AND I'LL BE READY AND WAITING FOR TOMORROW, TODAY.

OSCAR.

IT TAKES A LOT OF COURAGE,
TO FOLLOW YOUR HEART.
NO MATTER WHAT THOSE AROUND YOU SAY.

CHARLIE.

THE FEELING DEEP INSIDE YOU,
IS THE PLACE WHERE YOU CAN START.
DON'T GIVE UP OR TRY TO RUN AWAY.

JESSE.

YOU NEVER KNOW JUST WHEN,
YOUR MOMENT WILL ARRIVE.
BUT YOU'LL NEVER REACH YOUR DREAMS IF YOU DON'T TRY.

ALL.

TOMORROW'S ALL WE NEED FOR ANOTHER CHANCE TO DREAM.
DISCOVER POSSIBILITIES WE NEVER KNEW.
TOMORROW'S ALL WE NEED, SO HOLD ON AND BELIEVE.

AND I'LL BE READY AND WAITING FOR TOMORROW, TODAY.

COMPANY.

DREAMS CAN COME TRUE ANY DAY.
DREAMS CAN COME TRUE ANY DAY.

SOLOISTS.

BUT WE'LL NEVER REACH OUR DREAM IF WE DON'T TRY.

COMPANY.

TOMORROW'S ALL WE NEED FOR ANOTHER CHANCE TO DREAM.
DISCOVER POSSIBILITIES WE NEVER KNEW.
TOMORROW'S ALL WE NEED, SO HOLD ON AND BELIEVE.
AND I'LL BE READY AND WAITING FOR TOMORROW, TODAY.
AND I'LL BE READY AND WAITING FOR TOMORROW, TODAY.

SEBASTIAN. Wow! Thank you very much, all of you. That was...wonderful. Please give us fifteen minutes to talk, and we'll make our announcement shortly.

(Lights fade as **SEBASTIAN** *talks to* **CASSIE** *&* **JESS***, and the kids sit down together and wait.)*

(MUSIC: Scene Change)

Scene 7

(Outside, we see families waiting for their children. **HUGO** *is waiting outside – desperate to see how* **CHARLIE** *got on. We also see* **SPARKLE***'s mum bobbing up and down trying to find her daughter.)*

(All the children are leaving and buzzing as they leave.)

HUGO. Charlie!

CHARLIE. Hugo! What are you doing here?

HUGO. Wanted to see how you got on. Well?

CHARLIE. Didn't get the part, but I'm absolutely cool. I mean, I got down to the last day of auditions, and I've never done anything like this before! Maybe Mrs Jacobs was right. Maybe I do have something. But next time, I'll have some training under me belt! What have you got there?

HUGO. *(holding something behind his back)* Look what mum bought me? *(produces a pair of football boots)*

CHARLIE. AWESOME! Way to go, Hugo! Come on, let's run down the park and try 'em out! WAHOO!

(They run off)

*(***LILY, JEMIMA** *and* **SPARKLE** *are next out of the building, heading towards their families. As kids walk past* **JESSE***, they congratulate him for getting the part. He is clearly over the moon.* **LILY** *is met by both her mum and dad and brothers.* **LILY** *tells her parents she didn't get through just by facial reactions. Parents reply facially, worried she's disappointed)*

LAURA. Are you OK, honey?

LILY. *(linking one arm with her mum, and the other with her dad)* I'm just great, thanks. *(big smiles)*

(They walk away as a family.)

(Next we notice **ERIC** *waiting for* **JEMIMA***. He's looking the other way, reading a paper. He turns around when*

they all get closer, and once again, it's in the distance, so more visual than verbal. **JEMIMA** *looks at him, he looks intently at her. She's practically bursting out of her skin. She tells him she got the part. They hold each other's arms and jump up and down.* **JEMIMA** *points to* **SPARKLE**, *as* **JEMIMA** *will be sharing the role.)*

*(***JEMIMA** *says goodbye to the others, and we see* **ERIC** *makes a mobile phone call to* **JEMIMA***'s mum. He's happy, laughing, and hands the phone to* **JEMIMA**, *who is very animated and excited.)*

(We now hear them conversation…)

JEMIMA. *(in mid conversation, as they head home)* … I KNOW MUM! … thanks, I love you too…

(The conversation continues we just don't hear it.)

(Focus is now on **SPARKLE** *and her mum. We see* **LETICIA** *going absolutely crazy, making weird noises of delight, starts to move, not sure where to go, grabs* **SPARKLE** *to her chest and practically suffocates her…)*

LETICIA. My baby got the part!! My baby!!! *(to anyone else who'll listen)* 'Sparkle by day, Sparkle by night, Sparkle Moon is an audience's delight!'

This is the star of the show!! *(pointing to anyone)*

SPARKLE. Mum, did you not hear me, I'm SHARING the role? I'm only doing two shows a week.

LETICIA. *(dismissing what she said)* Sharing, shmaring… *(squeezing her daughter my the chin)* … you were born to be a star!!

(Flamboyantly throwing her arms around, we see **LETICIA** *madly looking for someone.)*

(As the final people head home, we see **LETICIA** *burst into the empty audition room, where the casting assistants are clearing up, and she makes a bee-line for* **SEBASTIAN** *on the other side of the room.)*

LETICIA. YOO HOO! SEBASTIAN?!

*(**SEBASTIAN**, who has his back to her, lifts his head in horror, and simply yells...)*

SEBASTIAN. SECURITY!

(Snap black-out – End of Act Two)

(MUSIC: Curtain Call)

*(After bows, music changes to **LIFE IS WHAT YOU MAKE IT**)*

*(SONG: **LIFE IS WHAT YOU MAKE IT**)*

COMPANY.

LIFE IS WHAT YOU MAKE IT,
SO LET'S MAKE IT FUN,
PUSH THOSE CLOUDS AWAY, HEY HEY,
TODAY'S YOUR DAY.

AND I'M TELLING YOU THAT
LIFE IS WHAT YOU MAKE IT,
SO LET'S MAKE IT SHINE,
YOU CAN MAKE YOUR WAY, HEY HEY,
TODAY'S EVERYTHING YOU WANT IT TO BE.

WOAH
OOH

NO-ONE KNOWS WHAT THE FUTURE HOLDS,
EVERY DAY IS DIFFERENT,
THAT'S THE FUN ABOUT IT!
AS YOUR LIFE SLOWLY EVOLVES,
MAKE EACH DAY COUNT,
JUMP UP AND SHOUT,
YOU MUST REMEMBER!

LIFE IS WHAT YOU MAKE IT,
SO LET'S MAKE IT FUN,
PUSH THOSE CLOUDS AWAY, HEY HEY,
TODAY'S YOUR DAY,

AND I'M TELLING YOU THAT

LIFE IS WHAT YOU MAKE IT,
SO LET'S MAKE IT FUN,
PUSH THOSE CLOUDS AWAY, HEY HEY,
TODAY'S YOUR DAY,

AND I'M TELLING YOU THAT
LIFE IS WHAT YOU MAKE IT,
SO LET'S MAKE IT SHINE,
YOU CAN MAKE A WAY, HEY HEY,
TODAY'S EVERYTHING YOU WANT IT TO BE.

WOAH
OOH
WOAH
YEAH! YEAH!

(Encore and play out, party atmosphere.)

*(SONG: **FEEL THE RHYTHM**)*

ALL.

FEEL THE RHYTHM OF THE MUSIC
MAKES YOU WANNA DANCE
WHEN THE BEAT GETS IN YOUR FEET THEN
YOU DON'T STAND A CHANCE
YOU GOTTA
SWAY YOUR HIPS AND MOVE YOUR FINGERS
TURN YOUR BODY ROUND
LOOSEN UP A LITTLE BABY
WHEN YOU HEAR THIS SOUND

COME AND FEEL THE RHYTHM EVERYWHERE
OH YEAH
WHEN YOU'RE FLYING HIGH YOU'RE NEARLY THERE...
WO OH YOU

GOTTA GIVE IN TO THE MUSIC OF THE RHYTHM OF YOUR SOUL
YOU GOTTA GIVE IN TO THE MUSIC AND LET IT TAKE CONTROL
AND TAKE YOU, TAKE YOU TO YOUR DREAM...UH HUH.
TAKE YOU, TAKE YOU TO YOUR DREAM.

KEEP YOURSELF TOGETHER WHILE YOU

TRY TO LET IT GO – NO OH
YOU'VE GOT TO SURRENDER
IF YOU WANT THE GROOVE TO FLOW
CLOSE YOUR EYES AND HEAR THE BEAT
TIL YOU JUST GO INSANE
WHEN YOU'RE BREATHING MUSIC YOU CAN
NEVER BE THE SAME

COME AND FEEL THE RHYTHM EVERYWHERE
OH YEAH
WHEN YOU'RE FLYING HIGH YOU'RE NEARLY THERE...
WO OH YOU

GOTTA GIVE IN TO THE MUSIC OF THE RHYTHM OF YOUR SOUL
YOU GOTTA GIVE IN TO THE MUSIC AND LET IT TAKE CONTROL
AND TAKE YOU, TAKE YOU TO YOUR DREAM...UH HUH.
TAKE YOU, TAKE YOU TO YOUR DREAM.
TAKE YOU, TAKE YOU TO YOUR DREAM.
AND TAKE YOU, TAKE YOU TO YOUR DREAM.

(Music continues as cast leave the stage leaving **CHARLIE, LILY, JEMIMA** *and* **HUGO** *(with football boots around his neck) all around their street sign.)*

*(**CHARLIE** climbs up to the sign and puts a big line with a whiteboard marker on the end of the N and adds an R to make 'DREAM' in front of the STREET.)*

The End

Lightning Source UK Ltd.
Milton Keynes UK
UKOW04f1512250816

281473UK00012B/113/P